The Law
of Gravity

OK. Everything had failed. There didn't seem to be any way that I could make my mother come downstairs. It was already mid-August and my father was due home in another week. There were just two possibilities open to me. The first was to admit defeat. Give up this crazy idea. If my mother had remained upstairs for so long, why should I be able to get her to come down in just a few weeks?

The other possibility was more drastic. I had to do something terrible that would make her come down....

Also in paperback from Beech Tree Books

Patricia Beatty
Wait for Me, Watch for Me, Eula Bee

Barbara Cohen
The Innkeeper's Daughter

Carolyn Haywood
Little Eddie
Eddie and His Big Deals

Isabelle Holland
Now Is Not Too Late

Johanna Hurwitz
Baseball Fever

Honoré Morrow
On to Oregon!

Judith S. Seixas
Living with a Parent Who Drinks Too Much
Living with a Parent Who Takes Drugs

George Shannon & Peter Sis
Stories to Solve: Folktales from Around the World

The Law of Gravity

a story by **Johanna Hurwitz**

illustrated by Ingrid Fetz

Beech Tree Books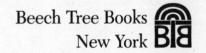
New York

William Morrow & Company, Inc.,
105 Madison Avenue, New York, New York 10016.
Printed in the United States of America
First Beech Tree edition, 1991

Library of Congress Cataloging in Publication Data
Hurwitz, Johanna.   The law of gravity.
SUMMARY: Margot's determination to get her obese mother
to leave their fifth-floor walk-up takes her into emotionally
deep waters.   [1. Mothers and daughters—Fiction.
2. New York (City)—Fiction]   I. Title.
PZ7.H9574Law   [Fic]   77-13656
ISBN 0-688-10498-3
10 9 8 7 6 5 4 3 2 1

To my mother,
who always ran up and down,
and the memory of my father.

1

"It was the best of times; it was the worst of times. . . ."

That was the first sentence of a book my father started to read aloud to me last year. We didn't get very far because he had to go on a concert tour, and then when he came home we forgot to continue reading. But the sentence stuck in my head, and it certainly was the right description of June 25.

It was the last day of school. The weather was hot and sticky, which suddenly reminded me of some of the bad things that come with summer. My shorts and T-shirt were clinging uncomfortably, and it was only 8:45 in the morning. Imagine how I would feel before the day was over after sitting in class. It was good that school was ending for the summer, because no one could pay attention to a teacher in that kind of heat. All the kids kept raising their hands to get a drink of water at the fountain down the hall. The water was only lukewarm and not at all satisfying. Yet ten minutes after you drank it you wanted to try again. Maybe this time it would be cold. It never was.

I was glad that vacation time had come around at last, and at the same time I wasn't. All of my friends (actually I have only two) were going to be away all summer, and I was staying home.

My friend Julie was going off to summer camp for the whole vacation. She went to camp last year too, and so she already knew what to expect. She had a whole group of camp friends and even a whole vocabulary of camp terms. For the past month all she had spoken about were "sleep-outs," "cookouts," "bunks," etc. My other friend was Esther, and until the day before I'd thought that the two of us were going to have a lot of fun this summer. We had planned all sorts of things, and I was really looking forward to vacation. But the night before she phoned me and she was all excited. Her parents had suddenly rented a cottage at the beach, and now she was going to be away for the entire summer. She was so thrilled that she forget to be angry that she would be sharing a room with her little sister, and she forgot all about the picnics in the park and the other things that we had planned together.

"Maybe you can come for a weekend," she said. That really didn't console me at all.

There are a lot of signs up in the buses and on the subways about New York's being a Summer Festival. My father once explained how the slogan is a clever advertising campaign to make people want to come to New York City in the summer, even though it is so hot then. If they stay in air-conditioned hotels and go to air-conditioned movies and air-conditioned theaters, maybe it's OK. But if you are on your own, without a friend in sight, the summer is a long, hot time in the city, and I wasn't happy about it at all.

So there it was, the best of times and the worst of times. If you were Julie or Esther, it was the best of times, and if you were me, Margot Green, it was the worst. The absolute worst!

When I got to my fifth-grade room, everyone was sitting around and talking to each other. I discovered that they were discussing the notice written on the chalkboard: *Summer Homework*. No one quite knew what to make of it. It was written in the very neat cursive that our teacher, Mrs. Eldridge, uses when she writes on the board. (When she writes a note to another teacher, her handwriting is easily the worst in the class.) It must be a joke, I thought. No teacher in the history of school ever gave homework over the summer.

Mrs. Eldridge came into the room. She had been down the hall speaking with another teacher. Everyone began shouting, "You can't give us homework." Mrs. Eldridge gave a big laugh—not a mean one, just a real hearty one—that showed that she had some joke on us. And then she explained.

"I'm going to be your teacher again in the fall!"

We all cheered at that. No matter how angry you got at teachers during the year, somehow during the last week you realized they weren't so bad. And all during the last few days I had been thinking that Mrs. Eldridge really had thought of some good ideas and that this had been a pretty good year.

We had gone on some interesting trips and not just to the Museum of Natural History. (If you live outside of New York City, a trip to the Museum is probably a thrill. But if you have lived all of your life in New York, then by the time you are eleven you have certainly gone to the Museum 279 times. Yet every year whatever teacher we have drags our class there, and when we groan and protest, the teacher says, "You don't know how lucky you are to have such a great museum in your city.") Well, we had visited a court, gone ice-skating, and shopped at the Job Lot Trading Mart (which is an enormous store with thousands of things for sale, and even if you have only a dollar saved up you can buy about ten different things with your money). Mrs. Eldridge was OK, and I was glad that we would have her next year.

"I really mean it about the homework," she said. When all the boos and shouts subsided, she explained. "Let me tell you about it. Why do you think it is good to study for ten months of the year and then for two months not do any reading or thinking at all?"

"I think," called out Fred Brandon. "I think what score the Mets are going to get in their next game and who is going to win."

"Human beings think every moment they are awake," said Mrs. Eldridge, paying no attention to Fred. "But it is important to think creatively. I want you all to make a summer project for yourself."

"What kind of project?" called out Julie. "There aren't any encyclopedias at my camp."

"You don't need encyclopedias to learn. Use your eyes and your ears. Study nature: insects, birds, plants, the sky at night. . . . Wherever you go this summer, there will be something for you to learn."

A girl in my class named Elise was traveling with her family across the country. They were going to the Grand Canyon. The only place I would get to would be the Grand Union—our local supermarket. I called out, "What if you aren't going anywhere? I'm spending the whole summer on 87th Street. I'm not going to study cockroaches." Everyone laughed, and I was sorry about what I had said because my mother is a good housekeeper and we don't have any cockroaches, which is quite a feat in New York City, where there are more people and more roaches than just about any other city in the world.

"You can study people; you can learn wherever you are."

Mrs. Eldridge turned to the board and started to make a list of suggestions: "Collect seashells and learn their names. Learn a new sport." (A lot of cheers here.)

"How about diving? I can swim, and this summer I'm going to learn how to dive," called out Maryellen.

"That's perfect," Mrs. Eldridge said. And eight kids had instantly chosen their summer project. I'd be lucky if I got to the beach a couple of times.

After that they all began raising their hands with ideas: cooking, knitting. One boy in my class had just gotten a unicycle for his birthday. He said he would learn how to ride it.

"Good. Good," Mrs. Eldridge said. "I want you to learn things from people and from life and from yourselves." That was really peculiar coming from the teacher who had made us write more book reports during the year than I could count on the fingers of both hands.

Mrs. Eldridge went out of the room, and everyone began talking at once. Of course Esther told me that she was going to collect seashells. "I could mail you some," she offered.

"I don't know what I'll do," I said. "But I have two long months to think about it."

Mrs. Eldridge walked back into the room,

lugging an enormous watermelon. That's why she is a good teacher. Just when you are mad at her, she does something unexpected.

In a minute, the melon was cut up into pieces, and there were twenty-seven kids and one teacher all chewing away on the cold, juicy fruit. Watermelon is one of the good things about summer.

2

I walked partway home with Julie, listening to her babble about how she would collect butterflies at camp. "There's a great nature shack, and I know the counselor will help me," she said. I left her at the corner of Amsterdam Avenue and walked home alone, crisscrossing streets to remain on the shady side. Some of the Manhattan streets have trees growing on them, right out of holes in the cement. Those streets are much cooler than the others.

In addition to keeping out of the sun, there is an art to walking the streets in the city. My father taught me to avoid those side streets where there are transient hotels—places where

people come and go and drunks or drug push-
ers are often standing about. For example,
86th Street is a wide cross street and better
to walk on than 85th. On my own street, I
know just about every face and feel very safe.
It is like a small town, especially last spring
when the Block Association held a street fair
to raise money for beautifying 87th Street.
Everyone participated. My mother didn't
come, but she baked three tins of brownies
and four dozen ginger cookies, which were
sold.

Two years ago my father played in a series
of concerts in Israel. Before he left, all his
and Mom's friends phoned and asked if he
wasn't afraid to go there. After all there is
always talk of war, and from time to time
bombs explode in streets or movie houses. Yet
after my father got back he told me that in
Israel everyone said, "You live in New York
City with your wife and daughter? How brave

of you. Aren't you afraid?" The Israelis calmly go about the business of living, and so do we here in New York. Some of my classmates have been mugged; so far I have been lucky and also very careful. I am always home before it gets dark, and our building is well maintained. The downstairs door has a good lock, and Mrs. Conklin, who always looks out her front window, is almost like a police guard.

My best protection, however, as I go about is O.J. He is my dog, a large, rusty-colored mutt we have had for the past six years. My father named him after the fruit-juice concession that is on Broadway, near our apartment. So he is called Orange Julius. Or sometimes, for short, O.J. I can't take him to school, of course, but whenever I go to the park he comes along. I guess I get my best exercise running with him in Riverside Park. And because he is big enough to scare off would-be muggers, Mom and Dad feel much better about letting me walk about the city streets. I guess you could call him my chaperon or even my nursemaid, just like the dog in *Peter Pan*.

When I reached my building on Riverside Drive, I began to climb upstairs. Some people think that all buildings in Manhattan have elevators. That isn't so. I live in a walk-up, and it is four double flights up to my apartment. Some days I just run right on up and reach the top without even thinking about it. But today was so hot that I was very aware of each step I took, and I moved deliberately. By then I was feeling pretty sorry for myself, and even the thought of my mother waiting in the air-conditioned apartment upstairs with a cold glass of lemonade didn't cheer me a bit.

I could just climb upstairs and stay there all summer, and no one would even know the difference, I thought. What's to come down for again, anyhow? This may seem like a weird thought, but I guess I got it from my mother. She went up once, and she never came down again.

Let me explain. My parents moved into this building when I was two years old. So even though I once lived somewhere else, I have no memory of it at all. The day we moved in here, my mother carried me upstairs. My father walked behind her, carrying a big bag of groceries. When they reached the top, my mother was red in the face and puffing for breath. (My father told me this. I can't remember.) She collapsed onto a chair and said, "Paul, I'm not going to be in a hurry to go down again. I like this apartment and will be happy to stay right here." Well, he agreed with her that she shouldn't go running up and down, and he didn't think anything of it when during the next few days she would ask him to bring groceries home with him when he returned from work. And the next thing he realized was that six months had gone by and she had never once gone downstairs. Now it has been almost nine years since we moved to this building, and she still hasn't come down.

One advantage of our building is the view we have of Riverside Park and the Hudson River. When I was little I would sit for ages watching boats move on the water and following the adventures of unknown children playing tag and riding bikes in the park. "That's the best TV in the world," my mother used to say. Even now I love the view, the changing seasons in the park and the sunset over the river each evening.

Then there is the advantage of living on the top floor; up another half flight of stairs is the roof. My mother discovered it the second day we were in the new apartment. She's big on cleaning things, so she brought a broom up to the roof and swept it; probably it was the first time it had been swept since the building went up in the 1890's. Then she had my father fix a broken guardrail, and afterward she took me there to get my fresh air every day. She brought up a couple of plants, and then a couple more, and since she has a wonderful green thumb, after a while the roof got to looking more and more like an annex to the park and less and less like a black, tarred rooftop.

My father is a flutist. I think his work must be fun—making music all day. He meets different types of people all the time. I guess that is why he is so tolerant of my mother's peculiar ways. He works strange hours, and since my mother doesn't complain, he is glad. He rarely is home for dinner, and often when he gets home I am already in bed. If he had been a pianist, they would never have moved into our apartment. How could you get a concert grand up four flights of narrow stairs? We have an old Steinway upright. It was brought upstairs in pieces.

We had been living in our apartment about six months when my father realized that if my mother stayed upstairs, I would be a prisoner upstairs too. And so he began taking me for walks, first with me in the stroller. Later we went walking all over the city on days when he didn't have to go to perform or rehearse. And sometimes he would take me on night walks too. I loved those walks the most. When the city is dark it is also very bright and lively, and we walked and knew just which stores kept late hours. There are two fruit stores in my neighborhood that are open twenty-four hours a day. Imagine wanting an apple at three o'clock in the morning and being able to buy one. Or half a pound of cherries.

When it came time to register me in kindergarten, my father was the one who filled out the forms in the school office and who got the medical forms filled out by the doctor. Most people don't realize that my mother never comes down. Julie and Esther know and have met her, of course, because they visit at my house often and have dinner and sleep-over dates with me. They love playing on my roof, and they don't ask about why my mother doesn't come to Open School Week. (My father comes instead.)

Once, just after Esther got her braces, she did ask me if my mother didn't ever have to go to the dentist. Well, she hasn't gone in all these years. Afterward the subject was like a private joke between us, just as we discussed Esther's sister, who is seven and an A1 nuisance. My mother cuts her own hair. I have the longest ponytail in my school because I won't let her cut mine. My mother also makes most of my clothes and all of her own. My father buys the groceries, or he did until this past year, when I began doing it. My mother hasn't been to a movie in years, but eventually she sees them all on TV. So, as she says, "What is there to go downstairs for?" She is happy upstairs and plans to stay there.

My mother isn't without friends. Mrs. Crawford on the third floor, and Bessie Ruth, who lives two blocks away and has known my mother since before I was born, visit with her regularly. Bessie is an honorary aunt and takes the title seriously, since she hasn't any children of her own. My mother's best friend from her days at Juilliard (that's a music school that she went to and where she met my father) lives in England, and she and my mother send letters back and forth. There are various other friends and acquaintances who drop by or phone often enough so that my mother can't be classified as a hermit. In fact, as I said, I have only two friends, so my mother is making out all right despite her seeming isolation. Years ago I can remember Bessie Ruth arguing with my mother about why she shouldn't shut herself off from the world. But these days Bessie, like my father, seems to have accepted her as she is. I haven't heard them discussing the subject for a long, long time.

A while back I asked my mother when she would go down and she said, "I'll come down for your wedding!" That was about two years ago. I've had a couple of boyfriends at school since, but I'm still a long way from getting married. So I guess she is staying put.

Thinking about all this, I reached the fourth-floor landing and rang the doorbell. No matter where she is in our five-room apartment, my mother always takes a couple of minutes to answer the door. She is rather heavy— well, actually she is fat—and she doesn't walk quickly.

The door opened and there she stood. O.J. was by her side, barking his welcome. I came in and plopped onto the sofa of the air-conditioned living room. I was about to tell her that I was going to stay upstairs with her all summer when the phone rang. As she moved off to answer it, I went into the kitchen. The apartment was a world separate from the street; clean, cheerful, and good-smelling, it was a pleasant home. I opened the refrigerator door and stood in the cool draft. Then I pulled out a pitcher of lemonade and began pouring myself a glass. My mother walked into the kitchen, smiling. "Well, how was the last day of school?" she asked. Then without waiting for an answer she said, "That was your father on the phone. He didn't expect to get home for supper this evening, but he will after all. So I'm going to need a couple of items from the grocery store. Will you get them after you finish your snack?"

I nodded. I really don't mind doing the shopping. In fact, it makes me feel important. So last winter I persuaded my parents to let me make it my special job. Shopping gives me a chance to try new products that are adver-

tised on TV, and sometimes there is a woman in the store giving away free samples of a new brand of pineapple juice or cocktail frankfurters. I took the list and a couple of bills my mother gave me and put them in the pocket of my shorts. I reached for O.J.'s leash, and he rushed to the door. "Back soon!" I called to my mother, and off I went. I was already down the stairs—you can always go down a lot quicker than you can come up—when I realized that less than ten minutes after I decided to spend the summer upstairs, I was already down. Well, I guess it had been an unpractical idea. I like coming down too much. There is too much going on that I don't want to miss. And if my mother had been down recently she would realize it too.

And suddenly, like a flash, into my head popped a marvelous idea for a summer project: I would make my mother come downstairs!

Dear Esther,

   You are so lucky that I could just turn green with jealousy, except that would make me look hideous. Write and tell me all about the beach. I keep imagining you jumping the waves and walking in the sand collecting shells. I can almost feel the sand between my toes when I think about it real hard.

   As for me, this is truly going to be the worst, dullest summer of my life. I wish I were a thousand miles away in any direction. I guess I'd settle for even ten miles away. Why am I stuck here, where there is no one to play with and nothing to do at all? At least if we lived out in the country somewhere, I could enjoy nature. Or if we lived someplace interesting, like Washington D.C., I could go sight-seeing. There is absolutely nothing left for me to do in NYC that I haven't done a thousand times before. I refuse to set foot inside the Museum of Natural History. If I must die of boredom this summer, I will do it outside of the Museum and not inside!

Only one good thing has happened. I got a brilliant idea for my summer project. I am going to work on my mother and make her go downstairs. I've always just accepted the fact that she stays upstairs, but now the time has come for a change. I haven't figured out how I will do it, but I have two long months and I'm sure I can succeed. After all, Mrs. Eldridge said we should study people, and so I think this is an original idea. I guess I am lucky to have an original mother! Anyhow, you won't have to bother sending me any shells.

Love,
Margot

3

My vacation began both quietly and noisily at the same time. Quietly because I walked about the apartment on tiptoe while my father silently practiced his music. Did you know that a musician can practice for hours without making a sound? He reads the music through again and again, so that he knows it in his head as well as in his fingers. And then it was noisy while my father practiced for hours the dissonant notes of the modern piece that he was going to give a premiere of. My father was preparing for another of his concert tours. He has been touring ever since I was an infant. It is a part of his life. This time he was going to Washington to perform at the Kennedy Center. Then from there he would be traveling to Florida and then north to Canada and finally to the West Coast.

My mother was very proud of him, and she talked the itinerary over many times. Yet she did not seem the least bit envious that he was going traveling while she would be staying home.

Not me. I wanted to go.

"Couldn't I come along?" I asked my father one afternoon during a break for lunch. "I wouldn't be a nuisance, and it would give me a chance to see some new places." I had a sudden image of drawing a map of North America and showing the places we went to as my project for Mrs. Eldridge. I had often dreamed before of accompanying my father, but this was the first time I began nagging about it.

"It's summer vacation, and I wouldn't miss any school," I reminded him.

"Not this year, Margie," my father apologized. "I'll be too busy with rehearsals, and I won't have any time to spend with you. We'll do it someday, I promise," he said. "You stay here and keep your mother company."

"I never go anywhere," I complained, feeling sorry for myself. "My life is A Tale of One City."

Actually this wasn't true. That very afternoon I went with "Aunt" Bessie and her husband, Joel, to spend a weekend on Fire Island.

I splashed in the ocean water, looked at shells but refused to collect any, and toyed with the idea of taking Bessie into my confidence. Perhaps she could advise me about how to make my mother come downstairs.

I decided against it. Anyhow, I could hardly get a word in all weekend. Bessie and Joel were going off on a chartered flight to Portugal the following week, and that's all they wanted to talk about the whole time.

Back home I took things easy and didn't worry about the project for Mrs. Eldridge.

School and September seemed too far away for me to be concerned. I stayed up very late at night, watching TV, and slept very late into the morning. Twice I slept till almost noon. Then the heat spell broke, and I had too much energy to sit about "rotting" as my father called it.

"Mom just sits about," I said, justifying my behavior.

"She certainly does not," my father answered. "Look at all she does: she tends the roof garden"—this year she had big boxes of soil and was growing tomatoes and peppers and a few other vegetables—"she is making you a winter coat, she cleans the house, she cooks meals for us and washes up after us. . . ."

"It sounds as if she's living in the eighteenth century," I said. "And you sound like a male chauvinist."

I was surprised when I said that because I really like my father, and he respects people and isn't that sort at all. He also has a sense of humor, and so instead of getting angry, he began to laugh.

"Well," he said, "I see that now you have been promoted to the sixth grade you are getting into women's lib. That's OK with me, but don't put down your mother if she doesn't want to join you."

Put her down, I thought. I don't want to put her down, I want her to bring herself down—down the stairs. I don't know too much about woman's lib. I only know the little bits and pieces that I have picked up from television programs and hearing other people talk. I suddenly got an idea, though, about luring my mother downstairs. But first I would have to raise her consciousness.

I decided to go to the library and do some reading on the subject, so that I would have some ammunition to work with. The public library in our neighborhood is one of my favorite places in the world. It is an old building, even older than my apartment building, and it also has a lot of stairs. There is a sign, *Pets Invited,* so I took O.J. along for company. We climbed the steps, and I was amazed to see that there were only three people in the whole place and two of them were librarians.

The third person was a boy from my school who had just graduated from sixth grade. I knew him by sight; his name was Joseph Bernazzoli, and everyone called him Bernie. I pretended that I didn't recognize him and walked over to the magazine rack. O.J.'s paws clicked on the tile floor, and both the librarians and Bernie watched us as we walked.

I wasn't quite sure how to begin on my project, and I thought that maybe I could find an article about woman's lib in *Time* magazine or something. As I stood there looking through the magazines, Bernie came over to me.

"Hi!" he said.

I looked up and said hello to him. Even though we had gone to the same school for our entire educations, it was the first time we had ever exchanged words.

"What are you looking for?" he asked. "Maybe I can help you?"

"Oh, I'm just browsing," I said. I couldn't possibly explain the whole thing to him. "Mrs. Eldridge, my teacher, gave the whole class a homework assignment to do over the summer."

Bernie laughed. "I'm sure glad I'm not in that class." He reached down to pat O.J. before walking away. "Look," he offered, "if you do need any help, just ask me. I know this place better than any of the librarians."

I sat down with a pile of *Time* magazines and a couple of copies of *MS*. My mother subscribes to *Better Homes and Gardens,* which is more her style. She is probably the only person in the entire city living in a walk-up apartment who reads that. *Time* magazine wasn't too helpful. I kept being distracted by reviews of R-rated movies and milestones in other people's lives. But *MS.* was more to the point. There was a long article about careers of several women: a pilot, a surgeon, and a conductor. The latter was a music conductor, not one on a train. Before my parents were married, my mother had studied voice. She wanted to be an opera singer. She still sings around the house a lot, but that's all. I closed my eyes and tried to imagine my mother in costume singing on an opera stage. I've been with my father to a couple of operas so I know what they are like. But though in my mind I could see her dressed as Carmen, my mother still was wearing her gardening gloves too.

I decided to pick out a book to read at home and then start to work on my mother at once. I walked over to the fiction section to select something.

Bernie came over to me. "What sort of books do you like?" he asked.

I giggled. "You sound like a librarian."

"Have you read this?" he asked, handing me *The Hobbit*.

I had heard about it, but I had never read it so I took it from him.

"I really recommend it," he said. "If you have to spend your summer in New York City like me, then the next best thing to a vacation away is to visit Middle Earth and the places that Tolkien writes about."

"Sold!" I said. "What else do you plan to do this summer?"

"I'm going to see all the Marx Brothers movies. There is an old movie festival and *A Night at the Opera* is opening tomorrow. Would you like to come?"

I was more stunned by the title of the film than by the idea that a boy was asking me to go with him.

We arranged to meet the next afternoon at 12:30 in front of the library. I checked out my book and hurried home with O.J., leaving Bernie alone in the library with the two librarians.

Sure enough, my mother was wearing her gardening gloves when I walked into the apartment. She had just weeded the vegetables, and she had a small bunch of radishes in her hand. "A couple of tomatoes are almost ripe already," she said proudly. "They are very early this year because I sent away for a new species, and besides it has been so hot."

"Mom, you should have been born on a farm!" I said. My mother was born in the Bronx, which is another part of New York City. She grew up in an apartment near the Bronx Zoo, and she could look out her window and see giraffes walking on a plain. It was the Bronx, but she says it looked like Africa!

"Tell me about when you were a singer," I begged.

"Oh," said my mother vaguely, "that was a long time ago."

"Did you ever sing before an audience?" I asked.

"Of course," she said. "I've told you all this before. I was in several competitions and won scholarships to music school. And I was a soloist with two different church choral groups. But my big dream was to sing with the Metropolitan Opera."

"So why didn't you keep on singing?" I asked.

"You were born, honey. And you are more important to me than singing."

"Oh, Mom," I said. "I'm a big girl now. You could go back to singing. I can take care of myself. Lots of women have careers when their children get older."

"I know," my mother answered. "But now it doesn't seem so important to me. Once I thought I would die if I didn't win each competition that I entered. Now I realize that winning isn't enough. I still love music and I can sing for myself. I don't need costumes and applause."

"So you sing to the tomatoes," I said with disgust. "That's stupid. You should be singing so that lots of people can hear you."

"Don't you know that studies show that plants thrive when people sing to them?" my mother said, laughing. "Margie, I'm happy as I am, and my tomatoes are happy too! Whatever you decide to do someday, I want you to be happy. And it's possible to be happy without being famous. You've heard Daddy play. If he was worried about fame he would never be happy playing in an orchestra and with small chamber groups. He would want to be a soloist, and he would be bitter if he didn't become one. But he loves music, and that is what is important. And that is what I learned from him."

I could see that I was getting nowhere. So I decided to try from another angle. "Well, don't you at least miss going to the opera or hearing Daddy play in concerts? Why don't you ever go to hear music played, if you really love it so much?" I could hear the sarcasm in my voice, yet my mother didn't get angry.

"I listen to Daddy practice every day when he is home. I listen to the radio and to all our records on the hi fi. I don't have to have an expensive ticket and a fancy dress to enjoy music better."

"Daddy can get us free passes," I said. But I knew I had lost this argument, and Mom was right in a way too. Sometimes concert audiences are dreadful. They come in wearing their best clothes and their worst manners. They whisper during the music or else they fall asleep. I've seen them many times.

"Come, let's go look at the tomatoes," she said. And then, irony of ironies, she started humming an aria from *Carmen* as she led the way to the roof garden, still wearing her yellow-and-green gardening gloves.

Dear Esther,

I have good news and bad news. First the bad: my mother is impossible. I tried to convince her that she should resume her music career, but she doesn't seem the least bit interested. It is going to be a lot harder to get her downstairs than I thought. She is always busy on the roof or in the apartment, and she shows absolutely no desire to go down at all.

The good news is that I am not the only kid left in the city, which is certainly the way I felt when you packed up and abandoned NYC for the seashore. Do you remember Joseph Bernazzoli? He was in Mrs. Reynolds' sixth-grade class and played Groucho Marx in that funny play in the assembly. I meet him every time I go to the library. I guess he reads even more than I do. He has a thing about the Marx Brothers, and the other day we went to the movies and saw *A Night at the Opera*. Next week we are going to see *Duck Soup*.

I tried to get my mother to go to a movie with me, but she said she would wait till it was shown on TV. If anyone else said that, you would say she was cheap. My mother isn't cheap and she isn't lazy. I wish I knew just what she was thinking about when she says no all the time.

How many types of shells have you found so far? You may have to send me some yet!

Love,
Margot

4

I have a tin ear. That means that I can't carry a tune at all. It is unusual for a child of musical parents not to inherit any musical ability. Yet I do love to listen to music, and that, my parents say, is the most important thing.

"There are too many musicians in the world already," says my mother. "Who will be left to sit and listen?" So when somebody asks me which instrument I play, I usually shrug and say, "The phonograph." When I was young, my father's friend Jules Hirsch tried to teach me to play the violin. I loved touching the smooth, shiny wood of the tiny violin, and I would sit in my room fondling the smoothness of the instrument for hours. But I hated to practice. I couldn't bear the ugly sounds that I produced. At last Jules told my father that I wasn't ready. That was his nice way of saying he didn't want to teach me anymore. I was very relieved.

Then my father tried to give me lessons on the flute. Before long he saw I wasn't ready for that either. And so my official musical education came to a halt.

"Be patient. You'll be good in many other things. You'll see," said my mother. I'm still waiting. I'm good at my schoolwork, and I'm the best reader in my class. But I'm still waiting to see what I will be special in.

In third grade we all wrote poems for a class assignment. I don't know if mine was really the best, but my father set it to a little melody, which he played on the flute while I recited it. We recorded it on his cassette player, and I brought the cassette to school.

Miss Linski, who was my teacher that year, loved it, and she played it for all the teachers and for the principal. Maybe I'll be a songwriter when I grow up.

In the meantime, I love to listen to music. Several times a year my father has an evening of informal chamber music at our apartment. Jules always comes with his violin, and his brother Martin, who is a dentist but plays the cello, always comes too. The other players vary. Usually there are five or six performers. A woman named Nancy Beethoven, who also plays the violin, comes sometimes. I always wonder if she became a musician because of her name. She told me that as far as she knows she is not related to *the* Beethoven.

There is always a small audience made up of the husbands and wives of the performers, and sometimes a few other people come too. Somehow we all fit into the apartment. Orange Julius lies quietly on the floor, occasionally beating the rhythm with his tail. He enjoys the music too.

My mother always bakes fabulous cakes, and after the music everyone eats and talks for hours. It is a lovely time, and usually I look forward to these musicales.

When Martin Hirsch reaches our door, panting for breath and holding his cello, he always says he will never come again. It is a standing joke, and he repeats it as he collapses into the nearest chair. My father says he would really love to be a professional musician, but he became a dentist because he wanted to get married and have a family. He was afraid that he would not be able to support himself otherwise. I imagine that when my father and Jules go off on their concert trips, Mr. Hirsch must be sorry to have to stay home filling holes in people's teeth instead of filling concert halls.

My parents celebrated the Fourth of July by holding one of their musical evenings. Be-

fore the music and during the coffee time, my
father and Jules spoke at length about their
coming trip. The more I heard the names of
those faraway cities like Atlanta and Sarasota,
the worse I felt. I wanted to go away. Why
can't I get away too? I kept thinking all
through the evening's music. I don't believe
I really heard a note of the music, only my
own angry thoughts. Even my mother's cakes
couldn't cheer me.

5

Two days later my father left on his concert tour. Before his departure he gave me his usual speech: "Be careful. Let your mother know where you are going. Take O.J. with you if you go to the park. Don't speak to strangers, etc. etc." My father once explained to me that even though he trusts me, New York is such a large city that it has more than its share of eccentric and strange people.

"I trust you, Margot," he said, "to use your head and keep out of trouble."

As a result of my father's being out of town a lot and my mother's being above the town, so to speak, I have much more independence than most of my friends. I don't abuse it, and so everything works out fine. Usually I am a bit sad when my father goes away. This time I was angry, because I felt I was being deprived of any adventure. I consoled myself with thoughts of working on my mother. I felt I would have a better chance without my father's presence. He accepts her as she is, and that is what he expects me to do too. I went downstairs with him and watched his suitcases while he hailed a taxi. I kissed him good-bye, and then I went off in the direction of the library.

Joseph Bernazzoli knew more about old movies, odd books, and fascinating things about New York City than anyone I had ever met. And it wasn't just because he was a year ahead of me at school. I would bet anything that he was an interesting person when he was in kindergarten. He was just that sort of person. When we were together I didn't think,

He is a boy, I am a girl. What would Julie say? (At her camp there is a constant boy-girl war, and I'm not sure if the object is to win or to lose.)

Bernie was always at the library when I went there. Finally I said, "What do you do? Live here or something?"

To my utter amazement, he said, "Yes." It turned out that his father was the custodian of the library and that he and his parents and his older sister actually did live in an apartment on the top floor of the library building. He told me that all the old library branches have apartments for the custodians, but that nowadays most of the men live elsewhere.

"When I was little, the kids used to tease me and call me a bookworm when they found out that I lived here," Bernie admitted. "But since I actually am a bookworm, I don't mind anymore." Then he told me that neither of his parents read very much, but that when he was little, before he even started school, he used to spend so much time looking at the books while his father was mopping and waxing the floor at night that he taught himself how to read. And of course by now he knew more about the library than any of the librarians. So it wasn't just an idle boast when he told me so the first day we met at the library.

I loved *Duck Soup*, and of course we immediately planned that the following week we would go to see *Room Service*. "What do you do when you aren't at the library or at the movies?" I asked. "Do you ever get fresh air?"

"Sometimes I go biking in Riverside Park," he said. "Want to come?"

"I can't ride a bike," I admitted with embarrassment. I explained that I lived on the top floor of a walk-up, and so I never owned a bike because there was no easy way to get it up and down the stairs.

"I keep mine in the basement of the library,

and I'll teach you how to ride," Bernie offered.

I was terrified at first. I've often seen fathers or mothers running behind their children when they are teaching them to ride a two-wheeler. The kids are always about six years old. I didn't want anyone to see me trying to balance myself. I was certain that not only would I fall and break or sprain something, I would probably wreck Bernie's bike as well.

However, he was very insistent, and so I let him help me up on his bike and pedaled hard as he instructed. In two minutes Bernie's face was red with exertion, and I had already crashed once, into a street lamp. But after he caught his breath, he insisted that I get back on the bike and try again. I could not believe anything could be harder than trying to balance oneself on a bicycle. We went around the block that the library is on two dozen times. I made a lot of enemies as I narrowly avoided old ladies, mothers pushing baby carriages, young children, etc. Finally Bernie said, "Come on. Let's go to the park, where we can get an open space for you."

"I don't think I really want to learn how to ride," I said. "What's the use? Even if I learn, I don't have a bike, and I'll forget how to ride right away."

"You can't ever forget how to ride," Bernie said, grabbing the bike with one hand and my arm with the other.

In the park it seemed a bit easier. There weren't as many people or obstacles about, and so I could concentrate on riding and not on avoiding people. I wondered if my mother was able to see me from our windows and if she would recognize me from the distance. I turned around on the bike to tell him that I thought I was getting the hang of it and discovered that he was about ten yards behind me, not holding on at all. I immediately crashed from shock. But I had learned to ride a two-wheeled bike!

"You only fell about three times," said Bernie, as I rubbed my sore knee. We were sitting on the grass, resting. I was feeling pretty good despite my bruises.

"Tomorrow let's pack a picnic and come riding in the park," Bernie suggested. "I'll ask my sister if you can borrow her bike." Bernie's sister was nineteen years old and had a summer job in a bakery. She went to college.

"We'll have to pack super good lunches to celebrate," Bernie said.

"What are we celebrating?" I asked him.

"You!" he answered. "Do you realize that you just did the impossible?"

"What do you mean?" I asked him. Now that I knew how to ride a bike it no longer seemed so impossible.

"You know, Newton's Law of Gravity: 'What goes up must come down.' You were up on the bike and you came down. But you didn't give up. You got back onto the bike, and in the end you didn't come down at all. You reversed the Law of Gravity."

"What goes up must come down!" The words stuck in my head. No matter what I had been doing during the past days: reading, going to the movies, even riding the bike just now, in the back of my mind I was thinking about my mother and how I would get her down. It seemed so impossible. After all the years upstairs, why should I be able to convince her to come down in just one short summer? I didn't think I would ever succeed with my project. But suddenly here was a scientific law on my side. She would have to come down! It was ultimately beyond her— or even my—control. What goes up must come down.

Dear Esther,

Stop! Don't send me any shells (in case you were getting ready to do so)!

Do you remember when Mrs. Eldridge told us the story of Sir Isaac Newton and the apple falling on his head, which gave him the idea for his theory of gravitation? Well, if apples come down, so will my mother. Suddenly I am convinced of it.

I learned to ride a two-wheeled bike, and I have gone riding a few times with Bernie. We rode to the Boat Basin in Riverside Park and up toward Grant's Tomb. Yesterday we got caught in the rain, and I thought about you and wondered what can you do at the beach when it rains. Can you still go swimming or do you have to stay inside, and if you stay inside, then what do you do? Bernie and I returned to the library (that's where we always start from) and spent the afternoon playing chess. I'm not any good at it, but at least I don't lose in three moves anymore. Now it takes ten to fifteen, and once we were even stalemated; that means that no one could win. And for me not to lose is as good as winning!

Today in the mail I got the letter from you and a postcard from my father from Toronto and one from Aunt Bessie from Portugal. The good thing about having people go away is getting mail from them. But I sure wish I could be the one to go somewhere and send the postcards instead of always being the recipient. Oh, well. Someone has to be home to receive the mail.

Love,
Margot

6

My mastery over that metal frame with the two attached wheels, the bicycle, was more than just a triumph of muscles over the laws of physics. It was a release from the six or eight blocks that had bound my life and limited my actions. True, Orange Julius and I could have explored farther. Yet somehow we never had. Now Bernie and I, he on his bike and I on the one that belonged to his sister, rode along the bike paths in Central Park and the ones parallel to the Hudson River in Riverside Park.

The smoothness of the motion, the breeze that the motion created, and my hair billowing out behind me as I moved were things I loved. When we got tired or thirsty, we would steer onto the grass and drop to the ground. It was a happy exhaustion, and I savored every moment of it. Bernie said I had much more stamina and better muscles than he had suspected. I realized that this was the bonus I had received from climbing up and down stairs so many times a day, for so many days over so many years. I even discovered with delight that when we pedaled uphill, Bernie got winded quicker than I did. After all, the library had only three stories, but my apartment was on the fifth floor.

There were always other people riding on the bicycle paths, and everyone waved and grinned at one another. It was wonderful, and I was thrilled to have joined the club. My father phoned two or three times a week. When he called from Sarasota on his way to still another music festival, I reported on my latest accomplishment to him. He immediately promised that when he returned home we would go shopping for my own bike. He said he was sure I could store it in the basement without any problem. I wondered why we never had thought of that before.

Meanwhile, however, Bernie's sister was very generous, and I used her bike several times each week. Bernie and I packed picnics and explored every corner of both parks. Our days followed a pattern. Wednesdays, when the film changed, Bernie and I always went to the movies. Other days we might exercise O.J. together in the park. Bernie envied my being able to own a dog. His mother has an allergy, and so he can't have any furry or hairy pets. He has two tanks full of interesting-looking tropical fish in his apartment, but you can't talk or play with fish the way you can with a dog.

Mrs. Eldridge would have loved Bernie. He

was never at a loss for something to do. His whole life seemed to be filled with projects. He was always learning new things and interested in going to new places, like little museums that I had never heard of before or historic houses that he read about in books. Bernie insisted that I go with him to the Museum of Natural History, and even there he found new exhibits that I had never noticed before.

One day I complained to Bernie that I wanted to travel to other places. "I wish I could have gone off with my father," I told him.

"OK. Pack a picnic, and I'll take you out of New York," he said.

"Out of the city?" I marveled.

"Out of the state!" he said.

So the very next day, picnic in hand (or rather knapsacks on our backs), Bernie and I set off. He wouldn't tell me where we were going, only that I would be home in time for supper.

My mother had been so relieved that Bernie and I were going somewhere by bus and not on the bikes that she had quickly given me her permission. Whenever my father is away on a concert tour, my mother feels very responsible for me. I have to give her a minute-by-minute accounting of my time. When my father is home she doesn't worry nearly so much, though I may go to the same places and do the same things.

When I told her that I wanted to go on a picnic with Bernie, our third for the week, she had said, "All right. But invite him to come and have supper here tomorrow. I want to meet him, since you two have become such good friends."

I extended the invitation to Bernie as we stood on Riverside Drive, waiting for the bus that would take us to the mystery location.

When I was little I used to wonder if you could follow the Drive all around the world and come back to where you started. It must have been in first grade, when we talked about Columbus and how the earth is round. By now, of course, I know that the Drive does not extend very far, but I thought about it as we waited for the bus.

We took the bus that picked up passengers on the east side of the Drive. And then we rode in a northerly direction. I looked out the window and watched the street numbers get higher and higher. "This bus doesn't go to the Bronx, does it?" I asked.

"No!" Bernie laughed. He was enjoying the mystery that he had created.

The bus took us farther and farther uptown. Suddenly Bernie said, "This is our stop."

Puzzled, I got off the bus. Not far away I saw the girders of the George Washington Bridge, which connects Manhattan with the State of New Jersey.

"Oh! We're going to take a bus across to New Jersey," I guessed.

"You're almost right," said Bernie.

We didn't take a bus at all. We walked! I had never known that you could do that. There is a narrow pedestrian path, along which we walked. It was exciting to cross the bridge as we looked down on the Hudson River below us. There was a breeze, and after a short while I was able to ignore the sound of the traffic that was running next to us.

"I wish we could bike across," commented Bernie, "but they don't permit it."

The view was spectacular. There was no question in my mind that from that angle and that height New York City was very beautiful.

"This is nothing. You should come across this bridge at night," said Bernie. "There are lights on the bridge and lights on the buildings, and they shine out in the darkness."

Suddenly Bernie slowed his steps. "OK," he

said. "Close your eyes." I couldn't imagine what he was planning. I swayed slightly with my eyes closed, he took hold of my hand, and we walked about a dozen steps. "All right. You can open them now."

Facing me was a large green sign with white letters: *Welcome to New Jersey.* "Now you can't say that you haven't gone anywhere this summer!" And Bernie laughed. "Let's take a rest," he said.

We sat down half in New York and half in New Jersey. There were many cars whizzing past us in both directions, but no other walkers in sight. We sat on the bridge, looking down on the water. There were several motorboats and even a few sailboats gliding along. Then Bernie reached into his knapsack. He took out two peaches and a deck of cards. We ate the fruit and played a game of Spit, Bernie kneeling in New York and I sitting Indian fashion in New Jersey, slapping the cards onto the bridge. I won the first game and Bernie the second. We would have played another game but a breeze came up, and suddenly the two of clubs blew off the bridge. We watched it float gently down, down, down to the water below, obeying the law of gravity.

It would have been fun to throw all the cards off the bridge, since the deck was no longer of any use to us. But we were both too ecology-minded to do a thing like that.

Bernie read my thoughts. "Fish don't play cards," he said.

"Not even Go Fish?" I asked.

"Especially not that one. My little cousin Anthony will love to play with these cards. He won't care if a card is missing." That was typical of Bernie, practical and thoughtful. No wonder I was proud to be his friend.

We got up, and I brushed the dust of New Jersey off my jeans while Bernie brushed that of New York City off his. Then we continued west across the bridge. We went down a flight of stairs at the end and walked along the Palisades. We picnicked overlooking the river from the Jersey side and hiked a bit along the rocks.

"Your mother is a great cook," Bernie said, finishing the oversize lunch my mother had packed for me.

"Wait till you come for supper," I said. "This is nothing."

To my mind, the best part of our lunch was the wild raspberries we picked off a bush we discovered by chance. To think that they had grown there and waited for us to come and find them.

I wondered if my mother could possibly plant raspberries on our roof. Wouldn't that be something!

7

I should have known that Bernie would like my mother. He was fascinated by our rooftop and spoke to her at great length about mulches and other things related to gardening.

"Where did you learn about that?" I asked him. After all, he had lived in the city all his life.

"I read about it in a book," he explained simply.

"There is a fantastic display of roses at the botanical gardens," he told my mother, when he admired her climbing roses. "Have you seen them?"

When she admitted that she hadn't been to

the botanical gardens since her childhood in the Bronx, Bernie immediately said, "Why don't we all go? It isn't too long a ride on the subway. I went last summer with my sister. You would love it, Mrs. Green."

I held my breath. For one second I thought Joseph Bernazzoli was in one single attempt going to succeed where I had failed. I thought that he was going to complete my summer project for me. I didn't know whether to be pleased or not. I wanted to be the one to make my mother come downstairs.

But the next second my mother said, "That's awfully sweet of you, Bernie. Maybe sometime you and Margot could go. I don't need any other roses. This little bush gives me enough pleasure to last a lifetime."

I found myself feeling very disappointed that Bernie had not succeeded. Would I have felt just as disappointed if she had said yes? I didn't know.

Anyhow, as a result of this exchange, I confided in Bernie a little later, when my mother was in the kitchen, and told him what so few people I knew were aware of—that my mother never goes downstairs. He was incredulous. No wonder! He spent his whole life running up and down the library stairs and going to more places in New York City than anyone I had ever met. He couldn't believe that my mother didn't want to go everywhere and see everything too.

Then he said something that really shocked me.

"Listen, Margot. I don't want to hurt your feelings or insult your mother, but I think I know why she stays upstairs all the time. She is just about the fattest woman I have ever seen. She is probably too embarrassed to let anyone see her."

Bernie's words stunned me, and I looked toward the kitchen, where my mother was preparing our meal. At that moment the woman in the kitchen looked different from the way she had looked a minute before. When you see someone every day of your life, you don't really see them after a while. Although I know what my mother looks like and I know she is heavy, still I never had seen her as *that* heavy till then. Bernie's words seemed to have inflated her like a balloon, and she suddenly grew bigger before my eyes. Of course she didn't change at all; it was my looking at her as if I were seeing her for the very first time, the way Bernie had when he walked into our apartment this evening, that made the difference.

All through supper I kept looking at my mother in this new way. The loose-fitting caftan she wore couldn't hide her immense body. I watched her slow, deliberate movements. Bernie's words certainly made sense. My mother's size must be the reason that she didn't want to go downstairs.

Bernie kept talking all through the meal. He explained why seeing the Marx Brothers on television wasn't satisfying to a real fan. He didn't like the commercials breaking in all the time, and he resented the cuts that were often made in the films. It was good that he spoke on and on, because my thoughts kept leaving the dinner table.

If I could make my mother go on a diet, if I could help her lose weight, then she wouldn't be self-conscious about her appearance and she could go out all the time. In fact, if she weighed less, the effort of climbing up and down the stairs would be much easier for her. It was frustrating to sit and watch my mother eat and at the same time try to think of a way to make her go on a diet. I was relieved when the meal was finally over.

That night, lying in bed, I tried to form a plan. If there was no food in the house, my mother wouldn't be able to eat. It was as simple as that. You get fat from eating, and if you don't eat, you get thin. I was so excited with this new project that I couldn't fall asleep. I imagined how my mother would look minus twenty, thirty, and forty pounds. After a while I heard the chimes of the church clock up the street. It was eleven o'clock. My mother turned off the television set in the living room, and I lay still. I had an idea. I would wait until she was asleep and check the food situation. I wanted to know just how much food was in the refrigerator and cupboards at this very moment.

It seemed forever until the twelve chimes of the church clock announced midnight. The house was silent, and I got out of bed. There was really nothing to be nervous about. If I was discovered I could say that I wanted a midnight snack. The only problem was that my mother would probably want to join me. The moment I sat up, Orange Julius, who had been sleeping on the rug at the foot of my bed, wakened. Always the watchdog, he followed me into the kitchen.

I closed the door before I turned on the light and then opened the refrigerator. Inside was a box of eggs, a piece of meat loaf on a dish covered with aluminum foil, a piece of cheese, yogurt, and the leftover salad. I took a bite of the meat loaf and fed the rest to O.J. He swallowed it in two large gulps. For a moment I considered whether O.J. and I should try to eat all the food, but the thought made me feel nauseous and wouldn't have done any good. My mother would refill the refrigerator again anyway.

So I closed the refrigerator and turned to the cupboards. They were filled with various canned and boxed food: three cans of corn, two cans of tomato juice, a box of noodles, six boxes of jello, a box of crackers, a can of grapefruit sections. What a lot of food there was. Too bad I couldn't feed it all to Orange Julius.

Then I would have a thin mother and a fat dog.

Feeling discouraged, I got back into bed and thought about how I could cut down on the food supplies in the apartment. My mouth tasted funny. I always brush my teeth before I go to sleep, and I missed the minty after-taste of the toothpaste. The faint onion flavor in my mouth seemed strange and unpleasant. I thought I would never fall asleep. I envied O.J. his clean conscience. The moment I was back in bed he lay down and was instantly asleep.

I heard the church clock chime once, but I didn't know if it meant twelve thirty or one o'clock or even one thirty. I fell asleep before I heard it chime again, so I will never know what time it was.

8

As a result of my night's adventures, I slept later than usual in the morning. When I returned to the kitchen, there was my mother sitting at the table eating her breakfast. Smiling her usual good-morning to me, she looked up from eating her eggs (two of them, fried, sunny side up), an English muffin (with butter and strawberry jam), and drinking a cup of coffee (with milk and two spoonfuls of sugar).

"What would you like this morning, honey?" she asked. My mother isn't from the dry-cereal-out-of-a-box school of breakfasts. When she says what do you want, she really means it.

I could have chosen eggs or pancakes or French toast, etc., but I settled for half an English muffin with a glass of orange juice.

"Mom," I said, "don't you think you should go on a diet?" I admit I wasn't very subtle. However, despite my lack of tact, she didn't get angry. "You wouldn't recognize me if I were skinny," she said.

"It would be good for your health if you lost some weight," I said. "And you would really look great."

"Honey, I've looked like this since you were born. My health is just fine, so don't worry about me." As if to spite me, she poured herself another cup of coffee.

She slid a grocery list across the table to me. "After you finish eating, would you please pick up these things for us?"

I looked at the list: flour, sugar, yeast. Mom loves to cook and she is a fantastic baker. I knew I would suffer if I pushed this diet business, but it seemed the logical way to get her to come downstairs. So I tried again, "Mom, you aren't going to bake today, are you? It's so muggy out!"

"You're out of the house half of the day." She laughed. "You won't feel a thing, and besides I'm going to make your favorite cinnamon buns. Then if you and Bernie go on a picnic, you can take some along."

"No, thanks," I said. "I don't think we're going on any more picnics this week." It was sort of a lie. We probably would. Bernie's sister had a half day off from work on Friday, and she had promised to take us to the beach if the weather was good.

I picked up the list, pocketed the five-dollar bill my mother handed me, and said, "See you later." On the way out I took O.J.'s leash off the hook, and off we went. By the time I reached the downstairs landing I decided to give O.J. a quick walk and bring him back home. Then I would discuss the situation with Bernie.

As usual, he was sitting in the library reading when I walked in.

"What's new?" he asked, grinning when he saw me. It was only the night before that he had eaten supper at my house, so he couldn't really expect an answer.

"I left my mom eating away," I answered gloomily. "She'll probably gain two more pounds before I get back home with these groceries." I waved the list at him.

"Don't buy them!" said Bernie.

"I always buy the groceries," I explained. "It's my job."

"Well, you could starve her out," said Bernie.

I think he was only half serious, but it was the only thing I could do. I knew my mother wouldn't starve if I didn't hurry home with the shopping order, but it would cut down on her food intake. So I said, "What shall we do today?"

Bernie suggested that we go to a museum, since it looked like rain. I used the library phone, which isn't meant for the public, but Bernie was special, and since I am his friend I've become special too. I called my mother and said that I wouldn't be home till midafternoon and hung up quickly before she could ask about the groceries.

Bernie and I took the crosstown bus to the Metropolitan Museum of Art. In addition to rooms and rooms of paintings, there are ones with old-fashioned costumes and furniture. We found the bed that Claudia slept in in the book and the movie *From the Mixed-up Files of Mrs. Basil E. Frankweiler.* I admitted to Bernie that it had always been my dream to spend the night at the library. "But you do it every night," I complained, "so it's beginning to lose its excitement for me."

"I sleep upstairs in a modern bed," said Bernie. "If you slept in the library, you would have to sleep on the floor or take all the books off a narrow shelf to make a place for yourself. And if you made any noise, my father would come running downstairs immediately. But in the dark, you wouldn't be able to read any of the books. So what's the point?" So much for my fantasies.

I still had the five-dollar bill in my pocket (along with the grocery list), and so I treated Bernie to lunch in the Museum cafeteria. Usually we paid for ourselves everywhere, but today I was feeling reckless. If I didn't spend the money, I would have to buy the groceries on the way home.

Around four I arrived home. I don't have my own upstairs key as my mother is always home to let me in. Climbing up slowly, I wondered how she was reacting to this first sign of rebellion I had ever shown. We've always

been very close, my parents and I, and I couldn't remember a time when I had not done exactly what was expected of me. My mother let me in, all smiles. On the kitchen table was a half-empty carton of groceries. "I phoned the store with my order," she explained, "and they just delivered the things. It really is very simple, and we could do it all the time, if you don't want to shop."

"Oh no, Mom," I said. "I just couldn't do it today." I went into my bedroom to get the five-dollar bill I had in my bank, left from my birthday money, to replace the bill I had broken at lunchtime.

The battle was lost before it even began. If my mother was ever going to go on a diet and lose weight, she would have to plan it herself. Obviously I couldn't starve her out when she could phone for groceries. She could phone the delicatessen, the ice-cream shop, the pizza parlor. . . . They all made deliveries. As fast as I disposed of food she could replace it. And no matter how determined I was to carry out my project—"operation gravity"—I knew I would never have the guts to cut the phone wires.

"What's for supper?" I asked.

Dear Esther,

Things are going rotten. My mother isn't even a little cooperative about this business of going downstairs. Sometimes I think if I don't succeed in getting her down, I will be trapped in this city forever. After all, I'm sure my father would have agreed to both of us accompanying him on his concert tour. Or at least he might have let me join him for part of it if he knew my mother was going up and down and could manage without a life-support system (me). Who would walk the dog if I weren't here? And who would bring up the mail from the box in the lobby?

The strange thing is I haven't the slightest idea why my mother wants to stay up in the apartment all the time. I've been thinking about your family and mine and how different we are. At my house we are all pretty close, yet we don't talk as much as your family. When I go to your house, every-one is always speaking at the same time. I love the way your mother waves her hands about when she talks. My mother speaks with her hands too, but in a different, quiet way. She uses her hands to work in the garden and to do needlework. My mother sings when she works, or she hums little melodies to herself, but she doesn't say a great deal.

There is so much sound in my apartment—music, dishes clanging, the sewing machine running, the phone ringing—that I don't think I ever noticed before how little my mother speaks. Maybe it is because my father is away and Orange Julius is not able to say anything to me either. When I am with Bernie, we talk all the time. Then when I come home I want to speak more with my mother, but somehow we never learned how to talk with one an-other. Isn't that weird? And all the time I want to ask her why. There must be a reason for her staying upstairs.

I went to the encyclopedia at the library, and I copied down the law of gravity. It said, "Every particle of matter attracts every other particle of matter with a force that varies directly as the product of their masses and inversely as the square of the distance between them."

What does that mean? It's all so complicated. If only it said every particle of *mother*. But I think it means that I am exerting a force on my mother, and the closer we get to understanding one another the better the chances are of my bringing her downstairs.

It is so confusing. Maybe I should just ask you to pack me up a bunch of seashells and be done with it already.

Love,
Margot

9

"Look," Bernie said, "I could think of a dozen ideas for a summer project. Why don't you give up on your mother and do something else?"

"No!" I said stubbornly. "There must be a way. It isn't right for her to shut herself away from the world. I must make her come downstairs."

"Well," said Bernie, "I agree it's pretty strange that she stays upstairs all the time. But she sure seems happy. She's a lot happier than most of the people down on the street. I think you should leave her alone."

"If *your* mother was upstairs, what would

make her come down?" I asked, ignoring Bernie's comments.

"My mother goes to visit my grandmother almost every day. She lives on 104th Street," he said.

"That's my problem." I sighed. "I don't have any relatives except my parents. My grandparents are all dead, and both my parents are only children. There are no relatives to visit."

"Say, if your mother had a baby, she would have to come down and go to the hospital," suggested Bernie.

I laughed.

"Let's brainstorm this thing," Bernie said.

"What's that?" I asked. Bernie knows so many more things than I do that sometimes I feel quite stupid. But he never shows off his knowledge.

"We'll make a list of anything that comes to mind—even if it seems crazy. That way we might come up with a super idea."

He ran over to the librarian's desk and returned with a sheet of paper and a pencil. On the top he wrote:

Ways to Get Mrs. Green to Come Down
1. Have a baby
2. If the building was on fire
3. If she needed an operation
4. If Margot was dying in the hospital
5. If there was something important going on in the street
6. If somebody important was downstairs (like the President or the Queen of England)

"No," I said. "I don't think she would care about them. Maybe famous opera singers like Beverly Sills or Joan Sutherland. She likes opera."

My interruption cut off our list making. Neither Bernie nor I could think of anything to add. We looked over the items on the list one by one and realized that they were not valid suggestions. For example, I couldn't set my building on fire. I couldn't even call in a false alarm and scare my mother into thinking there was a real fire. Both actions were against the law. I would probably wind up in jail.

"True," agreed Bernie. "But if your mother missed you enough, she would want to come down to visit you in jail." He was joking.

"I don't want my mother to get sick," I said, looking at the next entry on the list, which was for her to have an operation. "And *I* don't want to get sick either."

"What you need is just a small, temporary emergency," agreed Bernie.

Then I remembered something that happened at school last fall. Caroline George had just walked into the classroom when Greg Sanchez picked up a full can of paint that had been left in our room by some workmen. He

swung the can to pretend to spill the paint on Caroline, and, to his amazement and Caroline's and everyone else's too, the lid flew off the can and Caroline had instantly been covered with light green paint. It ran down her hair, looking like a cap on her head; it was on her face and on her eyeglasses; it was on her clothes, her skin, her socks, her shoes, the floor, the wall behind her. It was everywhere.

Everyone roared with laughter; it was like a scene out of an old slapstick movie. I can imagine Harpo Marx standing like that with paint dripping down him. The only ones who didn't laugh were Greg and Caroline and Mrs. Eldridge. Mrs. Eldridge took Caroline and Greg to the office, so we only heard about everything secondhand later. There is a shower in the custodian's room, and Caroline had to take everything off and wash. Then they found somebody's old raincoat that was in the Lost and Found and put it on her. And they phoned her mother and told her to come to school and bring some clean clothing. That's the point of this whole story. They phoned Caroline's mother, and within fifteen minutes she was at the school with the clean clothing.

Afterward, thinking about it, I had wondered what would have happened if Greg had aimed at me, not at Caroline. Would my mother have come to school with fresh clothing, or would she have stayed upstairs, giving the school some excuse or other about why she couldn't come? Would I have had to spend the entire day in an old raincoat? What would have happened? I was relieved that I hadn't been Greg's victim, but at the same time I regretted it. Had I been covered with paint, my mother would have had to make a fast decision, and I wanted to know what she would have done.

Having become such good friends with Bernie, I was able to tell him all this now. His reaction surprised me. Instead of saying, "Yes, she would have come down," or "No, I think she would have remained upstairs," he said, "Margot, you aren't being fair to your mother. If she was out of the apartment at work, she wouldn't be able to come to school for minor incidents like a little paint."

(Little paint! He never saw Caroline!)

"Once your mother leaves the house, you will really be on your own, a whole lot more than you are now. You better decide just why it means so much for you to have her come down. Obviously she cares about you. And if you care about her, maybe you should just leave her alone."

"You sound like my father," I told Bernie.

My father was due to return to New York City from his concert tour in another ten days. So I knew that if I was going to succeed without his interference, I would have to come up with something to bring her down fast.

"Listen," I said, "I think your first idea was the best. I'm going to work on my mother to give me a baby sister or baby brother."

Bernie looked at me strangely and said, "OK, but when is your father coming home?"

I blushed. Bernie may be a year ahead of me in school and very smart too, but even I know how babies are made.

Dear Esther,

You know how Fred Brandon talks about baseball all the time at school, and we always thought he was crazy? Well, believe it or not, *I* went to a baseball game yesterday. Bernie's sister and her boyfriend took us to a game at Shea Stadium. It's a long ride on an elevated subway to get there, and all the way Bernie was drawing diagrams on pieces of paper to explain the game to me. It sounded terribly confusing, but once we got to the stadium and the game began, I caught on to what was happening and even caught the baseball fever. Imagine, I got so excited at one point, when the bases were loaded and someone hit a double, that I spilled my cup of soda all over Bernie's sister. But she was so happy about the way the game was going that she didn't get angry, and her dress dried up fast as it was a hot day. The Mets won 7-4. I must have brought the team good luck, because they told me that the Mets had lost their last five games!

I have a new plan to work on with my mother. I'm all excited about it, but I won't tell you what it is just yet. I'll keep you guessing!

Love,
Margot

10

So far nothing I said seemed to make any difference in my mother's behavior. I hadn't been able to convince her to resume her singing career, and I hadn't been able to make her go on a diet. This time, I decided, I would be more subtle in my approach.

So that evening I took out the photo albums with the pictures of me as a baby. Mom came and sat down on the sofa next to me when she saw me looking at them.

"I sure was cute, wasn't I?" I asked. I didn't feel that I was bragging. It is hard to identify with a two-year-old that you can't remember being.

"You were the sweetest little thing," my mother responded. We turned the pages of the album, ooing and ahing over little Margot aged six months, learning how to walk at a year, and posing in the roof garden at the age of two. My favorite picture was one of me sitting at the piano at the age of one and looking as if I were actually playing. The prodigy Margot seems to put even Mozart in the shade, but of course it is just a picture!

"Do you ever wish that I was still a baby?" I asked my mother.

"No," she said. "Those days were lovely, but I like you as you are."

"I wonder what it would be like to have a baby sister or brother," I mused aloud.

"You would probably fight all the time the way you told me that Esther fights with her little sister," she said, dismissing the subject.

I didn't press on. I had an idea. I would borrow a baby from someone and bring it to our apartment. Then when my mother saw it, she would remember again how it was when I was an infant.

I tried to think who I knew with a young baby. None of our neighbors had young children. There is one family on the ground floor with children aged three and seven, but they were too old for my plan. I wanted a real *little* baby.

The next afternoon, at the library, I asked Bernie if he knew anyone with a young baby that I could borrow. He thought of his various cousins and second cousins, but none of them lived nearby. Suddenly he remembered, "You know Mrs. Gordon, the reference librarian?"

Of course I did. She only worked part time in the afternoons, but I spent so much time in the library these days that I knew everyone. Sometimes Bernie and I would go out and buy sandwiches or sodas for the librarians' lunch. Other times we helped straighten the volumes on the shelves. We were rewarded by being shown brand-new books, which we were the first in the neighborhood to read, and a couple of times they gave us leftover cake from their coffee breaks.

"Mrs. Gordon has a little son, less than a year old," Bernie told me. "She brought him into the library once when her baby-sitter was sick. And he stayed behind the desk and in the staff lounge all afternoon."

"Fantastic!" I said. "Do you think she would let him spend an afternoon at my house?"

"Ask her and find out," said Bernie sensibly.

I went straight to the desk where Mrs. Gordon was sitting. "Mrs. Gordon," I said, "I was wondering if you would let me borrow your son for one afternoon."

Mrs. Gordon looked very startled by my request. Then she started to laugh. "Margot, you're kidding me. This library only lends books, magazines, and records. We even lend cassettes. But we don't lend out people!"

So I explained to her that I was very serious. "I have a special homework project to do over the summer, and I need a baby for a few hours."

"Well," said Mrs. Gordon, "it just so happens that my sitter told me this morning that she won't be able to come on Friday, and I was thinking of bringing Jason into the library the way I did once before." I could see that she was wondering if it was a good decision to let her baby stay with me.

"I will take very good care of him," I promised, "and Bernie will help me." I turned to Bernie, who had just walked over to the desk.

Good old Bernie! He quickly agreed that he would help take care of Jason, even though I hadn't asked him before. And I guess that is what sold Mrs. Gordon on the idea. After all, if you think about it, she really didn't know me well enough to trust her baby with me. But everyone in the library knew Bernie and his parents, so that seemed to make it OK.

I could hardly wait till Friday arrived, and in the meantime I wondered whether or not to tell my mother that I was bringing a baby to visit. In the end, I decided not to. I thought the element of surprise might add to the impact.

Jason Gordon was cute. Even though he was almost a year old, he was still quite bald and he had only one tooth. He was wearing a dear little sunsuit that looked like a sailor's outfit (if sailors wore short pants), and he was sitting in one of those umbrella strollers that can fold up. I pushed the stroller down the street and tried to imagine that Jason was my little brother and that I was taking him for a walk.

"Your mother is sure going to be surprised," said Bernie.

When we got to my building, I took Jason out of the stroller and Bernie tried to collapse it. It was stuck and not as easy to do as we had supposed. Jason began to cry.

"Look, Jason," I said, "I'm going to give you a ride in my arms," and I bounced him in my arms and began to trot up the stairs. At first he didn't feel too heavy. After all, I had been carrying bags of groceries up the steps for almost a year. But groceries never squirmed in my arms or kicked me. (Later his mother told me proudly that he already weighed twenty-two pounds! But at that moment he felt as if he weighed at least fifty!)

I had to stop at every landing, and Jason cried when I stopped moving. Bernie offered to take him and to give me the stroller in exchange, but Jason just kept on howling. By the time we reached my floor, he was really screaming, and my mother opened the door before either Bernie or I could ring the bell. She couldn't imagine who was making that noise.

It wasn't the scene I wanted to show her. I was standing, panting for breath, sweat dripping down my forehead, holding a screaming, red-faced monster. Even his bald head had turned bright red! Orange Julius accompanied the crying with loud barks!

"For goodness' sake, Margot," gasped my mother. "Where in the world did you get that baby?"

"Bernie and I are baby-sitting," I shouted over the yells. "His name is Jason, and his mother is a librarian."

My mother held out her arms and took the baby from us. "Come inside," she said, leading the way into the apartment. Ten minutes later Jason was happily crawling about the roof garden with a cookie in one hand and a table-spoon for digging in the dirt with the other. He was another boy from the one I had lugged up the stairs.

"Gee, Mrs. Green. You sure have a way with babies," said Bernie admiringly.

"I guess a mother never forgets," my mother said with a laugh. She seemed delighted with the little boy and followed him about the garden. Although she moved him from the direction of the tomato plants, she let him dig where the last of the radishes were growing.

Orange Julius walked about the roof sniffing suspiciously at this new and strange four-legged creature.

"It would be fun to have a baby in our family, wouldn't it?" I said, watching the scene.

"It would be fun to have a baby come and visit us sometimes," said my mother. "I think I am quite finished with diapers and all that, thank you."

"Diapers?" I remembered the bag that Bernie had carried on his shoulder with all of Jason's equipment. There was a bottle of juice, a couple of little rubber toys, and a supply of diapers.

"Do you think I have to change his diaper?" I asked my mother.

"It would probably be a good idea to check," she said, not making any move to help me. I waited for her to say that she would do it; she didn't. Instead she said, "This is good practice for you, Margot."

I tried to pick up Jason, and he began to kick and yell. "I guess he doesn't need to be changed just now," I decided quickly. When I put him down, he was happy again.

We stayed at my house for two and a half hours. After a while Jason began to rub his eyes and suck his thumb. My mother picked him up (he didn't fight her the way he had fought me), and she laid him down on my bed inside with a towel underneath him. She gave him his juice bottle, and he drank a little of it before he dozed off.

"You make it look easy," I complained. "Every time I touch him he screams."

"It isn't easy taking care of an infant," she said. "But it's worth the effort. I think eleven is a little young to begin baby-sitting, Margot. You ought to wait till you are a couple of years older. And you too," she said to Bernie, "even if you are older than Margot. I can't think why a woman would trust two youngsters like you with such a young child."

Knowing that I had talked Mrs. Gordon into the whole thing, I didn't say anything.

Bernie and I sat in the roof garden, playing a game of chess, which I lost as usual.

There was a slight breeze, and the leaves of the two trees that my mother was growing in immense pots rustled gently. There was a peacefulness about the roof garden that I usually didn't notice. Even when a police or a fire siren could be heard coming from the street below, there was a calmness up on the roof. I guess I took the place for granted.

My mother brought out a tray with glasses of lemonade and raisin cookies. If we had a baby, I thought, Mom wouldn't have time to make cookies or to tend the garden. It didn't seem worth upsetting our whole way of life just to get her to go downstairs. Going to a hospital to have a baby would be only a single trip. Afterward she would come back up and take care of the baby the way she had taken care of me.

Jason woke. Mom changed his diaper, thank goodness. And then Bernie and I took him back to the library. He screamed all the way downstairs and all along Broadway in his stroller. People looked at Bernie and me as if we were kidnappers.

"Bernie," I said, "I've changed my mind. It isn't a good idea after all. Even if she came downstairs to have the baby, I don't really want a baby."

"I can't imagine why you say that," Bernie called to me over Jason's cries. "Babies are such sweet, charming little creatures." But then he added, "Anyhow, Margot, I thought of something we forgot. Suppose she had a baby but didn't go to a hospital. I read an article in a magazine at the library about how lots of women are having their babies at home. It's modern to be old-fashioned, or something."

"I'm glad you told me before it was too late," I said crossly. Jason's crying was getting on my nerves.

We delivered Jason to his mother. She didn't seem at all concerned that he was crying, and besides he stopped the very minute he saw her.

"I hope you're able to finish your school project with Jason's help," Mrs. Gordon said. She handed a dollar to each of us.

Bernie was saving up for a pocket calculator, but I felt like blowing my money right away. "Come on," I said. "I'll treat you to an ice-cream cone with sprinkles. You worked for it, and so did I."

I waved good-bye to Jason. He was looking

very angelic again, sitting on the desk with all the library staff cooing around him. But he didn't fool me. "So long, Jason," I called.

I didn't want to see him again for a long time. Maybe when he was eleven years old, like me.

Dear Esther,

Sir Isaac Newton did his gravitation experiments with apples. If he had depended on my mother, he would have wound up with applesauce and no theories. As for me, I am at a dead end with my project. I think if you would send me one each of about a dozen kinds of shells, I could look something up about them in the encyclopedia for Mrs. Eldridge.

If I wasn't always worrying about my darn project, everything would be fine. You'll never guess what Bernie and I did yesterday when the temperature was 96 degrees. We went ice-skating! Honest! Not in Central Park, of course, the way you and I do in the winter, but in an indoor rink that is open all year round for crazy people who decide they want to skate in the middle of August. I found an ad for the rink in the newspaper and convinced Bernie to come with me. Isn't NYC amazing? I wonder if there are rinks like that in other places. I had a lot of fun, though I fell three times. Gravity was certainly working on me. My only regret was that I hadn't thought to wear mittens!

Love,
Margot

11

OK. Everything had failed. There didn't seem to be any way that I could make my mother come downstairs. It was already mid-August, and my father was due home in another week. There were just two possibilities open to me. The first was to admit defeat. Give up this crazy idea. If my mother had remained upstairs for so long, why should I be able to get her to come down in just a few weeks?

The other possibility was more drastic. I had to do something terrible that would make her come down. I guess I had known it ever since the afternoon Bernie and I had made the list. Obviously I wouldn't set the building on fire or hurt myself or anything like that.

But there was the unspoken possibility—I hadn't said it nor had Bernie—of giving my mother a small fright. Just enough to bring her down. If I didn't come home at suppertime one evening, what would she do? It would be a test of her concern for me, her love. At what point would she care enough to come down and look for me herself?

I didn't say another word about my plans to Bernie. I knew he would disapprove. He had cooperated with me and been really helpful with the baby business, but he would get angry if he heard what I was plotting.

The following Tuesday was a typical day of the summer. I did a couple of errands in the morning, walked O.J., and had lunch. Then I told my mother that I would be going to the library. That's all I said. But I knew she would assume that I was meeting Bernie and that I would be home between 5:30 and 6. I carefully did not say, "See you at suppertime," or anything like that. Just "good-bye" as I closed the door behind me. I wasn't going to lie, and I wasn't going to be home for supper.

I did, however, go to the library. It was an overcast day that looked like rain. So Bernie and I remained there, and that afternoon he taught me backgammon. It's much easier than chess, and after a while I was winning. "It's a game of chance more than skill," Bernie said with a shrug, conceding defeat. "I prefer chess," he said, but he readily agreed to continue playing with me.

By four o'clock we were the only people left in the library, not counting the staff. Mrs. Bernazzoli came into the room and asked Bernie to run out and buy a loaf of Italian bread that she needed for their supper. "Do you want to eat with us, Margot?" she offered. I declined the invitation, and Bernie said he would walk partway home with me when he went to the store. I agreed.

However, as soon as we parted ways, I doubled back to the library again. Once I had told Bernie that my secret dream had been to spend a night in the library. Tonight was going to be the night!

Since I had gotten to know Bernie, I had also gotten to know the library building a lot better. There were many doors in it that I had never seen open until I met Bernie. Closets, storage rooms, washrooms, staff rooms. The building was as full of rooms as Bluebeard's castle, and I had decided in just which one I was going to hide.

On the second floor was a room in which duplicate and triplicate copies of books were stored. I'd gone in there with Bernie a couple of times to find a title for one of the librarians.

Mrs. Harris, who was sitting at the desk, nodded to me as I came off the second-floor landing. I was such a common sight in the library that I knew if anyone was to ask her, she wouldn't remember if she had seen me before or after Bernie had gone out to the store. I walked over toward the shelves along the windows and then ducked down below the bookstacks and out of view. There was no one about to see me, but if there had been, I would have said I was looking for a book on a bottom shelf. I crawled toward the door of the storage room and slowly raised my hand to the doorknob. I turned it and the door opened. In a second I was inside.

This was Tuesday, which meant that the library would close at 5 P.M. Really, it was all too easy. There was no challenge, and so I had plenty of time to feel guilty about what I was doing. Only, happily, I didn't feel guilty at all. I had brought a canvas bag with me to the library that day. I often used it for carrying my books back and forth. Today it also contained some food: two sandwiches, a bunch of grapes, and a banana. I was prepared to stay till the library opened at 9 A.M. the next morning. There was a toilet and a water fountain near

145

at hand. It's a wonder to me that more people don't hide out in the public library.

I wasn't hungry, but I ate one of my sandwiches anyhow, because it felt good to be doing something secret like eating in a room where no one was supposed to.

To pass the time, I opened one of the books I had borrowed that day and began to read. There was a pair of windows in the room, and although the day had not been bright, there was enough light to read by for a long time. Once I heard footsteps outside the door, but mostly it was very quiet. Gradually I became engrossed with the story I was reading, and after a while I actually forgot where I was and the hard linoleum floor I was sitting on. I didn't notice that it grew darker or even that I dozed off.

Suddenly I heard sounds at the door, and they jolted me awake. I crouched in my corner and listened. I heard someone whistling, and

146

I thought at first that Mr. Bernazzoli must be coming to sweep up. Then I recognized the tune as music from the Marx Brothers film that Bernie and I had seen last week, and so I knew it was he. I held my breath as the door to the room opened, and the light was switched on. It hurt my eyes, the way a sudden light in a dark room always does. I wondered what time it was as I scrunched down, making myself as small as possible. In a moment Bernie would probably be gone and I would be safe.

"OK, Margot. Come out, come out wherever you are," Bernie called out in an annoyed voice.

I didn't say anything, but at that moment I sneezed. I guess seeing Bernie jump made it worth giving up my hiding place. He really went up six inches but came right down again. That's the effect of gravity for you.

"How did you know I was here?" I asked, crawling out of my corner.

"Your mother phoned to see if you had stayed for supper. She was worried and I got worried myself, so I came right away to find you."

"How did you guess what I was doing?" I asked.

"Well, it's not ESP, if that's what you're thinking," said Bernie. "It suddenly occurred to me that I had been smelling peanut butter all afternoon. So I figured that you had a sandwich on you and that you had decided not to go home for supper."

He looked at me angrily. "My mother's eggplant was first-rate. If you didn't want to go home, you could have stayed with us," he said.

"Listen, Sherlock Holmes," I shouted at him. "You know it wasn't supper out that I wanted." My voice faltered. The guilt I had managed to avoid all afternoon was suddenly catching up with me. "What did my mother say?" I asked.

Bernie just grabbed my arm and pulled me

out the door. "Come on. See her and talk to her yourself," he said. As we went down the library steps, I saw the big clock and noticed that it was 7:20. It only seemed later to me.

On the stoop in front of my building was a small cluster of people. The first thing I noticed was a police car and a couple of policemen, surrounded by nosy neighbors. In the center of them all, looking pale and oddly out of place, stood my mother. She was holding onto O.J.'s leash.

Suddenly O.J. began to bark, and everyone looked as he began to pull on his leash toward me. My mother saw me and gave a cry—it sounded like a bar of music from an opera scene, loud and clear and piercing the air—"*Margot!*"

12

"Margot!"

Everyone was looking at me and speaking at once. O.J. kept barking and barking, and though I heard all the voices, it was a few moments before I could separate them out and know who was saying what. The blinking light at the top of the police car stung my eyes worse than the sudden light in the library storeroom.

One of the policemen said, "Is everything all right? Were you molested or anything?"

And that awful word *molested* rang in my ears. How I hated myself. Is that what my mother had been thinking about when I didn't come home for supper? The enormity of what I had done engulfed me, and I hated myself and everyone around me: my mother, Bernie, the neighbors, the world. All I wanted was to escape into my bedroom and shut the door away from everything.

The next ten minutes seemed like ten hours. The policeman wrote out some details in a little notebook. He copied our address, and Mrs. Conklin, from the ground floor, answered his questions before my mother could even open her mouth. For a moment I wondered if the policeman thought that nosy Mrs. Conklin *was* my mother as she spelled out my name: "*M-a-r-g-o-t;* the *T* is silent," she explained proudly, as if she possessed some secret information about me and my family. Obviously she and all the neighbors were enjoying the drama of having a police car parked in front of our house. Police cars are always zooming past, but they rarely stop.

154

"Well, Mrs. Green," the policeman with the notebook said, turning to my mother. So he knew which of these women was my mother after all. "It looks as if everything is OK here. It usually is, but I have a teen-age daughter myself, so I know how you felt."

My mother nodded weakly; the color had come back to her face, but since her operatic greeting she had not spoken a word. Now she swallowed hard and said in a voice hardly above a whisper, "Thank you, officer. My husband is away, and I didn't know what to do. . . ."

"That's all right," the policeman reassured her, closing his notebook. "It's part of our job." I guess maybe he felt good that this call had ended happily, but I knew that I wasn't happy and neither was my mother. And this wasn't an ending for us but just a beginning.

He got into the car with the other policeman, and they drove off. The neighbors seemed reluctant to leave. They were like actors with bit parts who didn't want to go off the stage. But Bernie said, "Mrs. Green, do you want me to help you upstairs?"

My mother shook her head and tried to smile at him. "No. Margot and I can go up together. Thank you for finding her," she added.

And then finally my mother and I, and O.J. too, made our way slowly up the stairs. My mother stopped at every landing for breath, and we didn't say a single word to each other all the way to the top till at last I was safely inside the privacy of our apartment.

Somehow I got to my bedroom and flung myself face down on my bed.

"Why?" my mother demanded shrilly. Her tone of voice was one that I had never heard from her before. She was standing by the side of my bed. Her face, earlier so pale, was now red from the unaccustomed exertions of the evening, and her breath still came in short gasps. Her hair hung damply, wet with sweat. She looked as ugly on the outside as I felt on the inside.

I didn't want to look at her, and for a long time I buried my face in my pillow and kept hoping that I would wake up from this awful nightmare I was having. But it wasn't a dream, and my mother didn't go away.

Gradually her breathing resumed its normal pace, and she asked me again, "Why, Margot? Why didn't you come home tonight?" The tone of her voice was quieter now, more like what I was accustomed to.

"Don't ask me questions!" I said.

"Margot," she cried out. "What is wrong with you? Why are you so miserable? All summer you have been like two children. One minute you are full of new adventures and running about happily, and the next minute you are home again, looking at me as if I were some sort of freak." She paused for air before she went on. "You study me all the time. I notice even if I pretend I don't. One would think that you had never seen me before and that you were looking at a creature from Mars. What is the matter with you? Why do you act so strange?"

"Me, strange?" I cried out, sitting up in bed. "I'm the same as I ever was."

"And so am I," said my mother. "So what is the problem?"

"It's you," I accused her. "Why don't you act like other mothers? Why won't you go downstairs?"

The question was finally out in the open. It had haunted me all summer, but now I had finally said what I had been thinking all these weeks.

For a long minute there was silence. Then my mother sank down onto the edge of my bed, and she sighed.

"Oh, Margot," she said sadly. "I was afraid

that was the problem. I guess I knew it all along, but when one acts a certain way for a long time, that pattern becomes so much a part of one, like a wart or a mole on the skin that it isn't noticed. I always thought that you accepted me as I was. If we managed when you were three and four, then there couldn't be any problems now."

"But I can't understand. . . ."

"It's just the way I am," she said impatiently. "I feel very uncomfortable down in the street. Some people are that way. I can't help it. Oh, Margot, I've tried to be a good mother despite everything. I always thought I was doing all right until this summer. Now I can see that I've failed." As she spoke she began to cry.

"No, no," I said. "You are a good mother, and I love you just the way you are. But I wanted you to come downstairs. That's why I didn't come home tonight. I wanted to scare you, so you would come looking for me. And it worked. Only now I'm sorry I did it." I could hardly get the words out, because by now I was choking with sobs. "I just didn't know any other way to make you come down. You *are* a good mother. You know it," I pleaded with her.

I leaned over to hug her, and as my arms went around her and hers around me I knew I would always love her. I couldn't remember my anger of the early evening. There was something very noble in her face, and I wondered how just a few minutes before I could have thought that she was ugly.

"Margot, I was so frightened. I didn't know where you were. I called Bernie and the police. Then I ran downstairs to meet the policemen when they came. . . . Don't you ever do such a thing again," she scolded. "I was crazy with worry about you."

"Oh, Mom," I cried. "You know I will never

do it again. But what about tomorrow? Will you go downstairs with me? We could take a walk in the park together or go shopping or anything. Will you?"

My arms were still around her, so I could feel a shudder pass through her. "You mean, now that I've done it, will I do it again?" she asked. "I don't know, Margot. It seems so easy to you, honey. But for me it is the hardest thing in the world."

"But Mom! There is so much to see and do. At the beginning of the vacation I thought that I would stay upstairs all summer just like you. Only I couldn't, and I'm glad I couldn't, because I've done so many wonderful things. I've only just begun to do all the things there are to do, but you're not doing anything. You're locked away from the world like a prisoner."

"I don't feel that way," said my mother softly. "Maybe it's selfishness and escapism, but I've been very happy until now, and I always thought that I hadn't harmed you in any way by my peculiarity."

"Mom," I said. "You haven't *harmed* me." I remembered how I had once tried to make friends with a girl at school named Kim. I invited her home to play one day, and she accepted. When we reached the apartment door and O.J. came bounding out to greet us, Kim let out a shriek and rushed down the stairs. I ran after her, and when I caught up with her in the lobby, she shouted, "Why didn't you tell me you had a dog?" She told me that she hated dogs, and from that day on we were never able to be friends. Weeks later someone at school told me that Kim's mother was terrified of dogs too. *My* mother never passed on her peculiarity. I certainly wasn't harmed.

My mother went to the bathroom and returned with a damp washcloth. She washed my face as she used to do when I was a little girl. The very gesture made me start crying again. "Oh, Mom, I love you the way you are. You don't have to change. I just didn't understand, that's all."

"It's my fault," she said. "It's all my fault. But when your father comes home, there is going to be a change. The time has come for us to change our life. It will be hard for me, but I will try. We have been talking about it for a while now. You will be happier then."

"Mom," I said, "our life is fine and I am happy. I just wanted you to come downstairs. But really, it's all so stupid. It doesn't make any difference if you want to stay upstairs. You're just as good as the mothers who run up and down. You are better! Honest!"

I cried some more then and fell asleep with my head on her lap the way I sometimes did when I was very, very little. And my last thoughts were, "It's Mrs. Eldridge's fault that all this happened." But later, thinking about it again, I realized that no one was to blame. It was a no-fault situation. Physics assures us that what goes up must come down, and if I hadn't pushed so hard this summer, it would have happened someday anyhow.

There was still much I didn't understand about my mother and her unwillingness to come downstairs. The one thing I now realized, however, was that my mother didn't understand it well herself. Perhaps in time it would work itself out. In school we learn that all problems have a solution. But maybe life doesn't always work out so evenly. Maybe what we have to learn is how to live with the problems even if we can't find an answer for them.

I was relieved that this dreadful project that had burdened me all summer was finally over. I would never write it up, but at least I was finished with it.

Dear Esther,

Well, I have failed and now I give up! If my mother wants to stay upstairs, that's her business and why shouldn't she? I suppose I should be miserable that I didn't succeed with my summer plans, but I confess that I'm not. Anyhow, in between everything else, I've had a lot of fun.

Yesterday Bernie and I rode uptown to Grant's Tomb. We discovered a group of people there building a mosaic wall in the park, and we were invited to join them. Everyone can design a section and is given little pieces and chips of ceramic tile to use. I wish I were more artistic and could do something fancy. I just made a little flower, but someone made a taxicab, using yellow tiles, that looks terrific. When you come home you'll have to go and see it.

Today was too hot for biking, but Bernie

and I walked O.J. and we accidentally came upon a group performing the *Mikado* in Riverside Park. My mother would have enjoyed the singing. They seemed very good for an amateur group. And the Japanese style costumes were beautiful (but I bet they were hot for the performers to wear).

It seems to me that everywhere I go something interesting is happening. I guess one just has to keep one's eyes and ears open in order to discover all there is.

I'll have loads to tell you when I see you. One thing is certain. This summer wasn't boring!

Love,
Margot

13

My father was coming home! This had been one of the longest concert tours I could ever remember his being on. Sometimes he was gone for two or three days, and other times he was away for two or three weeks. But this year he had played in four different music festivals, one after another. There are other flute players who are more famous, but I think he is the best. And the number of concerts that he participates in increases all the time, so I guess the people in the music world are coming around to my way of thinking.

My mother and I spent all day getting ready for his return. I was suddenly aware that there had been an unspoken tension between us all summer. It had hung in the air, and the dissonance, though silent, was as real as the harsh tones my father rehearsed in some of his modern compositions. It was the absence of this unpleasantness that made me realize it had existed before. Now the air seemed to have cleared. After my awful night out I felt closer to my mother than ever before, and I kept hearing little Mozart melodies in my head. Even the noise of the vacuum cleaner, as I went over our already spotless apartment, couldn't drown out the melody of relief I felt. Orange Julius sensed the arrival of my father from all the heightened activity. My mother polished furniture and baked a blueberry kuchen.

I was terribly excited as I waited for the day to pass. A couple of times my mother hinted that my father had an important announcement. I wondered if another tour was coming up. At four o'clock I took O.J.'s leash, and he came jumping to me. We went downstairs and sat on the stoop in front of our building to wait. My father had written that he would be arriving around four, and I wanted to see him the very first second.

For once, as I went out the door, I felt no wicked urges to say to my mother in the off-hand manner I had adopted earlier in the summer, "Do you want to come down and wait with me?" I knew she could quickly think of a lot of very plausible reasons why she must stay in the apartment: the plane might be delayed, and my father would try to phone us; she had to baste the duck that was roasting in the oven, etc. If she wanted to come down, it was her business, not mine. The summer project seemed pointless to me now, and I was no longer certain why I had launched my attack on my mother in the first place. As I left, I noticed how her eyes were sparkling.

She had been singing operatic arias all afternoon, and I knew that even if she didn't go down to meet him, my mother was as eager as I for my father's return.

At the front of my building there are two cement blocks, one on either side of the steps leading up to the entrance door of the house. These blocks are like seats, and almost always someone or other is sitting there and watching 87th Street walk by. Mrs. Conklin spends a lot of her time there. When her children were younger, she would sit with the baby carriage and gossip with neighbors. Now her children run about on the pavement or play ball and make chalk pictures on the sidewalk, and she still sits there.

Happily, that afternoon, there was no one on the stoop. The entire street was relatively empty, and I didn't have to face any of the people who had been out there last Tuesday night when I came home so late. I knew that

if I told them I fell asleep over a book at the library, they wouldn't believe me—even if in part that was what happened.

I watched a stray cat go by. O.J. watched too, but he didn't pull at the leash as he sometimes did. He knew we were waiting for something else. One or two people walked by. I regretted that I hadn't brought my library book downstairs with me, but I didn't feel like going back up to get it. The time passed very slowly as it always does when you are doing nothing. At school, the worst punishment is to have to sit in front of the clock and do nothing for five, ten, or fifteen minutes, depending upon the nature of the crime committed. I've never had to do it, but I tried it out at home once to see what it would feel like.

I wished I had someone with me to talk to. I thought of Esther, splashing away at the beach. She had sent me several letters over the summer, which was nice. I love to get mail, but it's not the same as talking with a friend. As for Julie, she hadn't even sent me a post-card, but I couldn't blame her. From what she told Esther and me during the year, she was kept very busy at camp and had no time for letter writing except for the required weekly letter to her parents. My best friend these days was unquestionably Bernie.

I had been afraid to face him at first after my escapade at the library. But he must have known how I felt, because the morning after he came ringing *my* doorbell instead of waiting for me to go to the library (and I had decided that I wouldn't go). We spent the day at my house, helping my mother on the roof garden by moving some of the big planters about and doing other chores.

It had been Wednesday, the day the film always changed at the movie theater that was having the Marx Brothers festival. We had gone every Wednesday all summer. But that

Wednesday, Bernie said, "Let's wait and go tomorrow or Friday." That's all he said, but I saw how concerned he was about my mother. He wanted me to stay with her, and he wouldn't race off to *A Day at the Races* without me.

He is truly a good friend. I was sure we would still be friends in the fall when he started going to junior high school. This summer had been a time of truce when we didn't have to take sides, boys together against girls, fifth graders together against sixth graders. And Bernie is the sort that lives that way all the time. I wondered why we hadn't met and become friends before this. He certainly had helped make this summer special, opening my eyes to all the good times you could have without going off on vacation trips.

I started thinking about my mother upstairs. She always knew how to have a good time without going away too. She wasn't one of those mothers in the PTA who kept running into school every day and asking the teachers what they were doing. And yet she wasn't one of those uninterested mothers who just ignored you. Julie's mother never seemed to care very much about what Julie did. I knew my mother cared, even if she didn't come and see me in the class play last spring.

Just then Orange Julius began to bark loudly, and I saw that finally one of the many taxis driving down our street had stopped and my father was emerging from it. In a moment we were all entangled in a three-way embrace while the driver had to wait for his fare. It was a good thing that I was downstairs to meet my father, because he wouldn't have been able to manage all his luggage up the stairs alone. He looked very tan and trim. ("No one cooks as well as your mother, and so I always lose weight on a tour.") When my father finally was able to speak to me after O.J. had quieted down, he said, "I don't think

I have to bend down so far to kiss you now. You seem to have been doing some growing while I was away."

"As long as you still recognize me," I said.

My father handed me the smaller of his cases and his flute case, which he never lets out of his sight. He once told me that he even eats with it on his lap on the airplane. That was like an extra hug, my being given the honor of carrying the flute upstairs. I planned to tell him a lot of things on our way up the stairs, but despite the luggage he rushed up, followed by O.J., who was barking his arrival. I was in the rear and I said nothing.

My parents embraced at the door, and within minutes my father had changed into more comfortable clothes, and we were all sitting in the living room and talking. My mother and I heard all about the concert tours, who had played poorly and who had been brilliant. My father described everything from his hotel rooms to the gowns worn by the soprano soloists in a performance of Haydn's *Creation* he had attended. He didn't stop talking or asking questions. Even information that had been exchanged in phone conversations or in letters over the past five weeks had to be repeated, as if the impact was lost until it was told in person.

For dinner we had my mother's roast duck in orange sauce and rice and string beans (from our garden) and a jello mold. The blueberry kuchen was for dessert, and my father swore that he had gained five pounds just eating his homecoming dinner.

"Margot, I guess it's a good thing we live so high up and without an elevator," my father said. "Or else you would be getting fat from all this good food. I only wish you had a little more color. Look at the good color your mother has."

It was true. Although my mother doesn't go downstairs, she gets quite a suntan from working in the roof garden.

"Margot did a lot of biking in the park this summer," my mother said, smiling. "But most of her time has been at the public library."

I choked on my mouthful of food. That was the perfect opening for her to tell about my night at the library.

Instead, my father spoke. "I really think we have been selfish," he said. "We should have sent you off to a camp for the summer or something. I just thought that if I was going to be away for so long, it would be hard on your mother to be all alone. But I guess we weren't fair to you. Anyhow," he said, "next summer things will be different."

"I didn't want to go to camp," I said, and suddenly I burst into tears. I jumped up from the table and ran into my bedroom, closing the door behind me.

I thought my parents would follow after me. But they didn't. That made me feel even more like crying, and so I just lay on my bed, sobbing.

14

I must have dozed off because I suddenly woke about midnight, still wearing all my clothes. I got up and went into the kitchen. My father was sitting there at the table, reading through his accumulated mail. O.J. was at his feet.

"Hi, honey," he said. "Don't tell me that you are on West Coast time too."

"What do you mean?" I asked.

"Well," he said, looking at his watch. "It is 12:30 here, but it is only 9:30 PM in Colorado, and while I may be sitting in this kitchen in New York City, my body is acting as if it is still out West, and I can't get to sleep."

My father suggested that we take a walk.

It was a long time since we had taken a night walk together. We left a note on the kitchen table for my mother in case she woke up, and we took O.J. along on his leash.

I love the city at night. It is awake and asleep at the same time. Most stores are closed and houses are dark. But there are cars moving on the street and some people walking about, and I always wonder where they are going and what they are doing at that hour. I assume that they wonder about me too, although now that I am eleven it must look less strange to see me walking along the street at night with my father than when I was five or six years old.

I always did my most serious talking with my father on our walks. This evening I was sure he would want to know why I had been crying. I wondered what my mother had told him about my hiding out in the library. Before I could say anything, he started talking.

"Margot, I know our life is a bit funny."

"Funny?"

"Well, out of the ordinary. I don't work from nine to five in an office like the fathers of your friends. And your mother— Well, your mother is about the best mother in the world, but you couldn't call her conventional. She is strange too, like me."

"I like being strange," I said. I meant it too, even though a week ago that very strangeness had been upsetting to me.

"Well," my father said, "suppose we got a chance to lead a more normal life?"

"What do you mean?" I asked.

"I've been offered a part-time teaching position in the music department at Stony Brook. It may lead to full-time teaching, and even if it doesn't, it means that I would work on a more regular schedule. And I wouldn't be away from you and your mother on such long tours." He paused for a moment. "We might even move to Long Island if this job develops as I think it will."

"Move?" My mind began to whirl. I remembered the list that Bernie and I had composed of ways to get my mother to come downstairs. Neither of us had thought of moving.

"How could we move?" I asked. "Mom never comes downstairs. How could she leave her garden? I'm sure she wouldn't move."

"You're wrong there," my father said. "Your mother and I have been talking about this for some time, even before I went away. At first she was reluctant, but now she agrees that moving to a new community should be considered. We could rent a ranch house." He grinned. "Then your mother would be downstairs all the time."

I stopped walking and grabbed his arm. "Dad! Did she tell you what I did?" And then even before he could answer, I began telling him all about my summer project and how awful it had been. I listed all the things that I had done and what had happened. "I was

rotten," I admitted. "And you know? After all that, I discovered that when she came downstairs it didn't really matter. My life is exactly the same as before. I have no project to show for the summer."

"Life isn't like a magic show with amazing transformations," my father said thoughtfully. "You didn't really want your mother to come downstairs to change your life. You wanted her to come down to change her, and that's not for you to do. People must change themselves; they shouldn't be manipulated by others."

I thought about my father's words. "Do you think she will ever change herself?" I asked. "I think she is ready to try," my father answered. "It will not be easy for her, and we must continue to love her even if she fails."

"Oh, I will, I will. I do," I said.

"If we do move, it won't be for another year, at the earliest," my father said. "Can you find enough things to keep you occupied?"

"Oh, Dad," I said with a laugh. "In June I thought I would die of boredom. But the days weren't long enough this summer to do all the things I wanted." I told him about all the wonderful bike rides that I had taken with Bernie and all the places we had gone to.

"You know," my father said, "I felt guilty about leaving you in the city this summer and not sending you off to a camp, but it seems a far, far better thing I've done."

"What's that?" I asked.

"That's a paraphrase of the last sentence in the book by Charles Dickens that we never finished," he said. "It's a good thing you stayed here in the city."

"Oh, yes," I agreed. "It was a far, far better thing."

Dear Bernie,

I am having a great time here with Esther and her family. The beach is a nice place to visit, and I've even collected a lot of shells (for myself, not for Mrs. Eldridge).

One thing is certain—I spent more time in the library this summer than anyone else in my class. And I'm sure I'm the only one who worried about gravity and even looked it up in the encyclopedia. Yesterday I went to the library here in Long Beach with Esther, and I tried to find what else Sir Isaac Newton ever said. I looked in Bartlett's *Familiar Quotations* and I found this one by Sir Isaac:

> I do not know what I may appear to the world: but to myself I seem to have been like a boy playing on the seashore, and diverting myself in now and then finding a smoother pebble or a prettier shell than ordinary, whilst the great

ocean of truth lay all undiscovered before me.

I think it is a good thing that I didn't look for shells this summer, even if I'm not sure what I am going to write up for Mrs. Eldridge.

This has been the best summer I ever had.

I'll be home in a week, and I'll come looking for you at the library.

Your friend,
Margot